Our most sincere thanks to the basilica's staff for the attention and kindness they showed us during the writing of this book, especially to Míriam Martín, from the Press, Image and Communication department, for her help during the photographic work.

Fourth Edition

© **Editorial Kapitel**

Text: Jordi Bonet Armengol - José Mª Fuixench Naval
Photography: José Mª Fuixench Naval
Design and layout: Editorial team
Revision: Patricia Hueso Taulés
Translation: Andrea Regueira Martín
Architectural work © Junta Constructora del Templo Expiatorio de la Sagrada Familia
Photograph on page 15 © Junta Constructora del Templo Expiatorio de la Sagrada Familia
Printing: INO Reproducciones, S. A.
E-mail: editorialkapitel@gmail.com
www.editorialkapitel.com
Legal Deposit: HU-293-2015
ISBN: 978-84-937005-7-7
Impreso en España / Printed in Spain

**With the collaboration of
the Construction Board of la
Sagrada Familia Foundation**

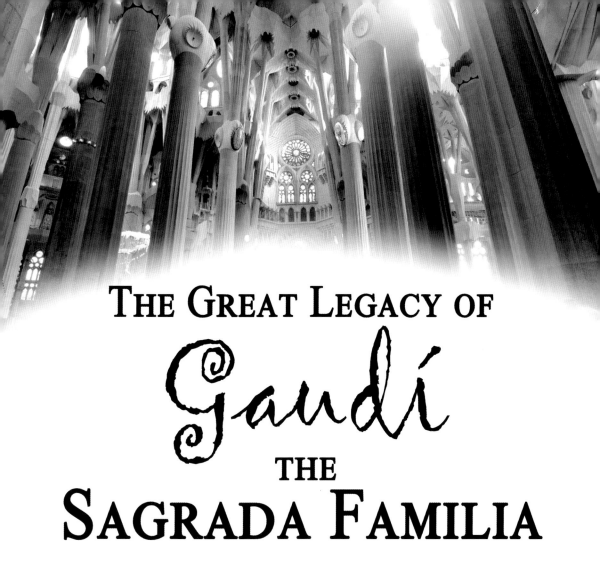

THE GREAT LEGACY OF
Gaudí
THE
SAGRADA FAMILIA

JORDI BONET ARMENGOL
JOSÉ Mª FUIXENCH NAVAL

Editorial Kapitel

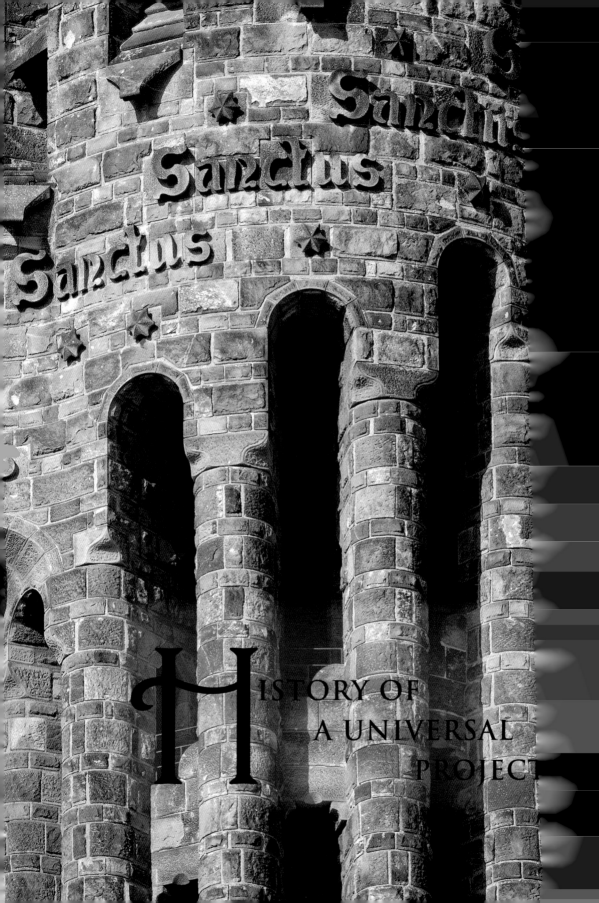

History of a universal project

Mr. José Mᵃ Bocabella, bookseller from Barcelona, was the temple's instigator.

People from all over the world will come to see what we're building", said the great architect Gaudí... and time proved him right.

It was the time of the Industrial Revolution, an innovation which Catalonia took advantage of in order to create an unexampled industrial network in a country, Spain, that was eminently agricultural. Such economic prosperity gave rise to social changes that favoured sponsorships and an artistic renaissance, but it also produced a recession of religious values.

A bookseller from Barcelona, Mr. Josep Mᵃ Bocabella, wanted to relieve that decay, and in 1866 he founded the "Spiritual Association of Saint Joseph Devotees". But his fervent mind held the idea of erecting an expiatory sanctuary — that is, one paid for solely with donations from worshippers— dedicated to Mary, Joseph and Jesus: *the Holy Family*. A decade later he acquired the privileged building site where he could make his dream come true and surround it by quiet gardens which, like a cloister surrounded by trees, would contribute to spiritual retreat on the monument's shadow.

The city's bishop, monsignor José Mᵃ Urquinaona, blessed the first stone of the future temple on Saint Joseph's day 1882 in that deserted place. That moment marks the beginning of the long journey of one of the most outstanding buildings of universal architecture.

The Sagrada Familia is the last great cathedral under construction in the world. Its unmistakable silhouette illustrates the book of universal architecture.

The original project was commissioned to the diocesan architect Mr. Francisco del Villar, who would draw the first plans in the neo-gothic style that was popular at the time. However, discrepancies with the Construction Board led to his resignation shortly after he started. His demands were such that the building's continuity was endangered due to high costs.

Shortly after that, this elevated task changed hands to a young architect from Reus. His projects revealed a distinguished origi

nality right from the day of his graduation, when the director of the School of Architects said: *"I don't know if we're giving the title to a madman or to a genius"*.

Antoni Gaudí, who was 31 years old, would soon completely change the original plans. He believed that gothic forms failed to reflect the design of the best of architects, the Creator. He would therefore adopt the laws of the Creator's own work; nature itself.

Gaudí conceived an extraordinary building which would not only revolutionise

The temple receives crowds of visitors every day.

When he was sixty years old, after having built Casa Milà and having finished his work in Mallorca's Cathedral after its bishop died, when the works in Colonia Güell's Church had stopped and his friends Eusebi Güell and bishop Torras y Bages had died, Gaudí dedicated the rest of his life to this temple.

Between 1921 and 1924 he aimed to solve the interior project completely: *"we are going to build a complete stretch of the inside to the tiniest detail".* The result was a plaster cast model on scale 1/10 that included modulation, geometry, proportions and geometrical laws. This model can now be seen in the basilica's Museum along with the final model of the bell towers.

These models, destroyed at the beginning of the Civil War, were restored, and from the study of their restoration it has been possible to discover the modulation and the simple geometrical formulas that he devised, and to build the monumental landmark faithfully; the columns with ramifications and the vaulted ceilings: a combination of ruled surfaces that make up his "New Architecture". *"The temple's naves will be like a forest in which light shines from the top, between the foliage",* explained Gaudí to the construction's visitors. When confronted with questions about the work's slow advance he replied: *"my client is not in a hurry".*

Several architects have led the monument's advances after Gaudí's death. As he used to think: *"big temples were never the work of one single architect".*

architecture on a structural level, but also on a symbolic level. There is no better structure than a tree, a reed or our own skeleton, and there is no better symbolism than that which flows from the spirit, he thought.

Until then gothic style was the one which gave way to the biggest temples. They were bright and clear, but in exchange they had to be clad in an armour of buttresses. Gaudí wanted to go one step further and, understanding that the best designs did not come from men's hands, he adapted the ruled surfaces so that the constructive elements themselves would be aesthetic as well as functional, resulting in a fully harmonious sanctuary. As he said, the Sagrada Familia *"is not the last of the great cathedrals, but the first one of a new era".*

Bread and wine are shown on the pinnacles.

Down:
Curious gargoyles cling to the apse's walls.

Mr. Jordi Bonet, the director architect who has spent the longest time in charge of this masterpiece, second only to Gaudí himself.

Mr. Jordi Bonet Armengol has been in charge of the temple's direction and is the *alma mater* of this informative work.

Born in Barcelona in 1925, he has been the church's director for nearly three decades, leaving his post to the new director Mr. Jordi Fauli at the end of 2012.

Doctor in architecture, he was been granted prestigious awards throughout his career, from which we can highlight the "Cruz de San Jordi", awarded by the Generalitat de Cataluña, and the "Civil Order of Alfonso X the Wise". Besides, he is commander of the Order of St. Gregory the Great. He received the award "Ciudad de Barcelona" twice, as well as the "Domènec i Montaner", "Gaudí-Gresol" awards and Barcelona's Medal of Honour.

Vital man as he is, his architectural career before he took on the temple's direction is far-reaching. He has used Gaudí's ideas in several types of buildings: homes, industrial buildings, churches, theatres, schools, auditories, etc. He has held the positions of general director of Artistic and Cultural Heritage of Catalonia, president of the Catalonian Royal Academy of Arts, and he was a Scout world leader. Several books, hundreds of articles and numerous conferences around the world about Gaudí's patrimony illustrate his career.

Under his direction Gaudí's geometries were deciphered —the plans had been destroyed during the war—, the columns' foundations were laid, the naves' columns and vaulted ceilings were built and, for the first time in the history of architecture, computers were used in the stone cutting machines, which greatly increased working speed.

Mr. Jordi Bonet gave the temple's keys to Pope Benedict XVI on November 7 2010, when the pontiff consecrated the Sagrada Familia, granting it basilica status.

Gaudí, The Genius

Nature was his main source of inspiration. His forms had never been used in architecture before.

ntoni Gaudí i Cornet was born on June 26 1852. He was the youngest of five children in a family of boilermakers from Tarragona's Baix Camp region. With a lot of effort, his parents could afford to send two of their sons to university in Barcelona.

There he studied a degree in architecture, working at the same time in order to be able to afford living in the Catalonian capital. He can't be described as a brilliant student, but he took advantage of his time at school to learn what the library had to offer him, thus deepening the knowledge he received from his professors. The future architect undoubtedly exhibited some uncommon characteristics as a student.

The first project he signed as an architect was for the Maratonense Cooperative, which shows his interest in ideas related to the working classes and their promotion. The building is now restored and open to the public as a space dedicated to the promotion of fine arts. Gaudi's nave with its wooden parabolic arches is still standing.

Europe was changing, and the Barcelona of the turn of the century was home to important industrials, like Mr. Eusebi Güell, who became interested in the architect after visiting the Paris Exposition and seeing a display cabinet for a glove shop designed by him. This would be the beginning of a fruitful personal relationship that resulted in important commissions under his sponsorship.

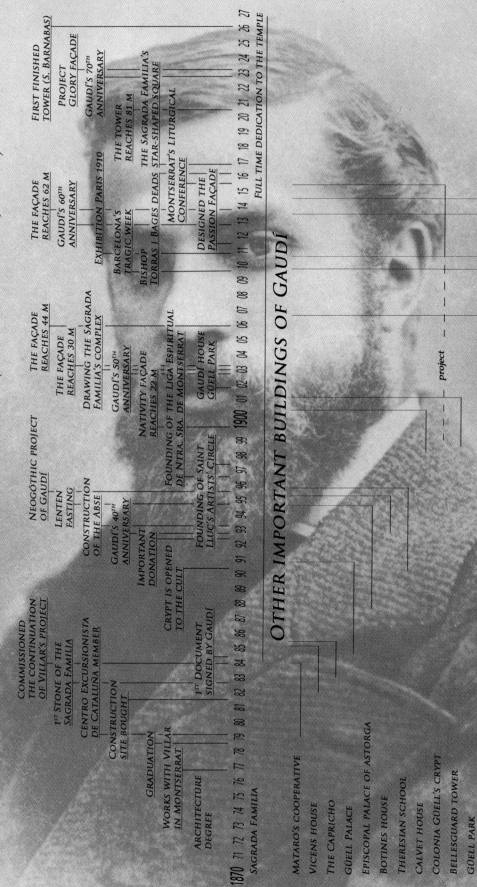

IMPORTANT MOMENTS IN GAUDÍ'S LIFE *(Reus, 25-6-1852 - Barcelona, 10-6-1926)*

OTHER IMPORTANT BUILDINGS OF GAUDÍ

Colonia Güell's Crypt was one of his main grounds for architectural experimentation.

A NEW ARCHITECTURE

His work before the 20th century goes from Casa Vicens (1879-81) to his first jobs for Güell. Outside Catalonia he designed a house called "El Capricho" in Comillas, Santander (1883-85), Astorga's Episcopal Palace (1889-93) and Casa de los Botines in León (1893-95) and in Barcelona the School of Saint Therese (1889-95) and Casa Calvet (1898-1900).

These projects were held in high regard by influential personalities from Reus, his hometown and then Catalonia's second biggest town; like Joan Baptista Grau, bishop of Astorga; Sant Enric d'Ossó, who has just been canonised and founded the order of Saint Therese; or architect Joan Martorell, who recommended him as Villar's successor in what would be the most important work of his life; the Sagrada Familia. Today Gaudí is the only architect in the world with seven buildings classed as World Heritage Sites by UNESCO.

Colonia Güell's Crypt

The crypt of the unfinished church from Colonia Güell was the most singular experimental laboratory, as we can see in its calculations and in the system that links and synthesises form and structure. Only an architectonic genius could offer these results using only simple materials and the

Mediterranean technique of *"maó de pla"* vaulted ceilings, which was documented as early as the 14th century and is still used in Catalonia today.

The leaning columns, the hyperbolic paraboloids from its vaulted ceilings, the use of *"trencadís"*, face brick, and a long list of architectural solutions and details are, along with the vast collection of documents that were used in its construction, object of study in order to gain a better understanding of Gaudí's procedures, as well as of the admiration that he raised in so many important contemporary architects around the world.

Güell Palace

This is the first building which was fully planned and finished according to Güell's taste, who totally trusted the architect. He built the underground stables along with its access ramps, the great brick pillars that support the vaults, and the façade, which features a double grille gate with the coat of arms placed between the parabolic arches. A design that came together with ingenious innovations, which were the result of a dialogue between owner and architect. Dialogue that would bring them closer together throughout the years.

First-rate industrials and artisans helped Gaudí's creative task with all sorts of solutions, details and materials, as great clients and exceptional architects do.

Gaudí traced a main floor used to greet distinguished visitors, with an imposing central hall that receives light from a svelte pinnacle. It's a space with great acoustics, feature shared with the chapel. It is followed by a great dining room with its corresponding toilets and, finally, a floor dedicated to family life that would house a large number of descendants. The top features a combination of chimneys and air vents.

The building was acquired by Barcelona's Council and first it would be used as the headquarters of the Museum of Theatre. Nowadays, as it should be with such an interesting building, it can be visited, and the restoration work sponsored by the Council is praiseworthy.

Casa Batlló

The transformation of an ordinary apartment building in Barcelona's Ensanche, was a great success, particularly when it comes to its façade. Its impeccable carpentry is accompanied by an extraordinary use of leaded glass egg-and-dart decorations in the main hall, together with the

Casa Batlló's osseous structures enrich its famous façade.

hues given by the exterior's luminosity, make this building stand out enormously in paseo de Gracia.

Gaudi solved the lower floor the contrast of the severity of the iron reticular gate that closes it. The spectacular roof, which resembles a dragon; its mask-shaped balconies; and the colours, which are full of fantasy, express the artistic freedom enjoyed by the architect.

It is important to highlight that a plaster cast copy of the altarpiece from the Batlló family's little chapel, with figures sculpted by J. Llimona, would be used to dominate the Sagrada Familia's crypt. A century later, the original was bought and the copy was donated to the parish church of Trempt when Josep Manyanet, founder of the Sons of the Sagrada Familia who came from this town, was proclaimed a saint.

Park Güell

The park, which was originally conceived to give Barcelona's citizens a garden city, was a failure. Its location, overlooking the Mediterranean, offered visitors magnificent views. The complex shows high quality, daring architectural solutions which were also economical thanks to the use of the building site's stone. There, the colour and movement from Gaudi's "New Architecture" are presented to us in their full glory, with Nature harmonically dominated by an artist's great skills. The use of *"trencadis"*, parabolic arches, the cutting of the stone and the formal richness it offers, along with Mediterranean vegetation,

Left:
In Batlló House, the dragon-shaped rood, symbol of evil, is pierced by Saint George's spear, tower-shaped with a cross on top.

Right:
Like never-ending cloisters, the porticos in Güell Park are in harmony with their surroundings.

elicit admiration for the skilfulness and originality of the whole complex.

Episcopal Palace of Astorga

It was a commission from Reus' prelate Grau shortly after he became bishop of Astorga. After the old palace had been destroyed in a fire, Grau granted Gaudí the project to build the new one in 1887.

The neo-gothic building failed to satisfy the public and the clergy, which led to Gaudí's resignation then the works were already under way, right after he had worked in the bishop's tomb, who had died in 1893.

School of Saint Therese

The building commissioned to Gaudí by Sant Enric d'Ossó —founder of this feminine educative order— is located in Barcelona's Ganduxer street. Over a century after its completion, the building is still used as a school. It features parabolic arches that make up a central courtyard and luminous classrooms arranged in lines, vertical slots, with face brick in the interior and facade. The roof, made with traditional elements and technology, constitutes proof of the architect's rationality.

The "Dragon Gate" guards Güell country house.

The Bellesguard Tower at the feet of the Tibidabo mountain.

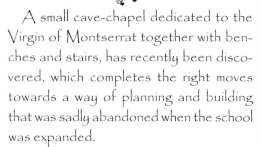

A small cave-chapel dedicated to the Virgin of Montserrat together with benches and stairs, has recently been discovered, which completes the right moves towards a way of planning and building that was sadly abandoned when the school was expanded.

Gaudí was asked to design the chapel but declined due to a disagreement with the religious order, whose members failed to grant access to the chapel to ordinary citizens.

Casa Calvet

Casa Calvet was built at the turn of the century. This magnificent five floor bourgeois house is located in the lower part of Ensanche, in Barcelona. In 1900 it was named the best building in the city by Bar-

celona's Council. The façade, built with ashlar from Montjuïc, combines a baroque look with modernist elements. Inside, the ground floor, which hosts the owner's offices, features a bright courtyard that takes advantage of the changing natural light and houses the staircase and the lift.

Countless pieces were designed by renowned artisans, from the most striking works in iron and stone, to the smallest ones, like the door's peephole and handle. Most of its furniture is also of great interest, as it was designed by Gaudí himself. Also noteworthy is the symbolism that alludes to the family, for instance the columns in the facade, which have big thread bobbins that represent the owner's career —he was a textile industrialist—.

Bellesguard Tower

It is an important residence commissioned by a traditional Catalan family; the Figueras family. Located on the slope of the Tibidabo mountain, it offers a view of incredible beauty, which is reflected in its name, Bellesguard, which means "beautiful view".

The owners bought the land when there were still elements and ruins from a palace that had belonged to king Martí I, last song of the Catalan dynasty. Using the land's own stone, Gaudi built a new mansion in a little over two years. It was neogothic in appearance and crowned by a svelte spire with a four-armed cross. Its long openings remind one of gothic windows from the best medieval buildings.

The stone roof over arches built with ceramic elements presents in its interior light combinations that astonish the visitor. On the outside, Gaudi reconstructed the walls and towers and built a great iron gate of astonishing remarkable and beauty to enter the building.

Casa Milà "La Pedrera"

In Casa Milà, Gaudi planned a high standard apartment building, with a car park accessible by a circular ramp and spacious courtyards and ventilation. Without master walls and with a free floor, dozens of aligned columns make the modification and distribution of space easier. An artistic interior design gives soul to the homes.

The façades have large openings and balconies are harmonically located in caps and joined by curved forms. With the use of cast iron banisters of different profiles he managed to make the whole evoke the waves of a calm sea made of stone.

The roof includes ventilation chimneys shaped like guardians, as well as windows that multiply themselves over a gently leaning surface. It is supported by countless parabolic arches made out of face brick that develop themselves in nearly parabolic curves, which results in a singular garret that grants structural stability to a complex that could have only been conceived by a privileged mind.

Litugic restoration of mallorca's cathedral

While Mr. Pere Campins, bishop of Mallorca, was visiting Barcelona, he asked Gaudi for advice about the refurbishment he was planning in the interior of the island's cathedral. He was so fascinated by his explanations that he commissioned the works to him.

Gaudi moved to Mallorca to take notes on the project and shortly after he presented the plans and a model made out of wood and plaster cast that captivated the canonry. Once it had been approved, Gaudi took part effectively in the restoration of this great example of Mediterranean gothic. He moved the choir stalls, which were placed in the main part of the nave, to the sides of the altar, which showed the tall chapel next to the apse and the royal graves. By doing this, he offered a majestic view of a gothic space that focused on a hanging canopy over the altar that dominates the cathedral.

Among other actions, the presbytery was decorated with ceramic facing, the baroque altarpiece was dismantled in order to be taken to the church of Santa Catalina, and the gothic altarpiece was moved to the vantage point gate.

The traces of Gaudís inventiveness can also be seen in the stained glass, which were made using a new technique, by superimposing glass, which allowed him to get a greater chromatic richness.

GAUDÍ AND "THE RENAIXENÇA"

It is important to note that Gaudí joined the cultural movement known as "the Renaixença", which implies a compromise in the promotion of Fine Arts by institutions and personalities of the time. This Renaissance also aimed to take back Catalan language and culture so that it could develop in a universal level. Gaudí, along with the playwright Guimerá, was present at the first reading of the poem "Canigó" by Jacinto Verdaguer, one of the most important writers in this movement. He also had a great relationship with relevant personalities like poet Joan Maragall, bishop Torras y Bagues, Prat de la Riba and other contemporary intellectuals.

He was a member of the "Catalonian Excursionist Centre", in which he took part actively; of the "Spiritual League of Montserrat's Mare de Deu"; and of the "Artistic Centre of Sant Lluc". As a leader, he visited monuments around the country to promote conservation of artistic heritage and he took part in the remodelling of its headquarters and in various acts of cultural relevance; from the decoration of the great gothic hall in the Lonja Palace, to his contribution in the Ciento Hall in the House of the City of Barcelona, although this failed to be carried out.

On June 7 1926, as the sun was setting, Antoni Gaudí was hit by a line 30 tram while he was going to pray at the church of Saint Felipe Neri, and despite how admired he was in the city, on that day nobody recognised the elderly man with a white beard who was lying on the floor. Three days later he died in Santa Creu Hospital, the hospital for poor people, just as he wanted.

His effort in the stimulation of faith through art granted him the nickname "God's architect". His process of beatification is currently opened.

GAUDÍ'S PERFECTIONISM

Gaudí wanted to make a dream come true, and he covered it in details that made it almost real. Details like arranging that trees to be planted in the parks surrounded the Church of the Sagrada Familia came directly from Palestine so that the temple would be impregnated with the aroma of the Holy Land.

When he conceived the Flight to Egypt scene, where Mary, Joseph and the Baby escaped from Herod's persecution, he needed a donkey to make the plaster mould before he had it sculpted in stone. Gaudí could have used the best donkeys in town, but he wanted an animal that would convey the fatigue caused by the long journey. From his window he could often hear a sandstone seller. When he heard her voice advertising her product he remembered that the woman always had a donkey pulling the cart that contained the goods. The animal was old like its owner, and it represented exactly what Gaudí was looking for. Gaudí gave her a price for the animal and she accepted, saying goodbye to her loyal companion in tears. The donkey's name was Margarida. Days after that she was shaved by a shearer and her body was greased with butter so that the plaster cast wouldn't stick to her body. But the animal was afraid of that strange treatment and it was impossible to make it stand still so, with the help of a canvas that went under her stomach, she was raised. Her old owner was also called upon to calm her down with whispers and caresses while the plaster cast was setting and she could be free again. Today we can see this donkey in the gate of Hope, with the Virgin and the Baby riding on her back. Margarida is small, she looks tired and her ears are a bit lowered... the exact expression that the genius from Reus was looking for.

Gaudí designed the Passion façade during a Maltese fever that brought him so close to death that he even had to write his will. When he could feel the agony in his own body, regardless of how weak he was, he knew it was the right time to draw that façade in a sketch impregnated with his own pain. A drawing that would allow death to be sculpted in stone and would reflect Jesus' suffering with breathtaking realism.

Regarding, the Annunciation scene, located in the Nativity façade, the constellations of the Zodiac are organised in the same disposition as they are on November 25, and they surround a 59-bead rosary that belonged to the architect's own mother.

For the scene the Death of the Just, in the Rosary chapel, he wanted to represent death in such a realistic way that he went to Santa Cruz Hospital to see if he could take the mould of a dead person. Right then there weren't any corpses, but the nuns told him that an elderly man who had no family was very close to the end. Gaudí chose to be with him during his last moments so that the man wouldn't be alone and he prayed with him. The architect to amazed the world with his inventiveness had a humanity of the same level. That elderly man was immortalised in the scene.

Barcelona, from the "Tree of Life" of the Sagrada Familia.

A Unique Temple

The presbytery has no altarpiece. For Gaudi the façades themselves are the altarpieces.

Right:
Under the canopy that gives shelter to the crucified Christ, the altarpiece is a big block of rock.

The Sagrada Família's silhouette is a symbol, a story sewn on the book of universal architecture. But the making of such an innovative building required many rehearsals. Fortunately, count Eusebi Güell, Gaudí's friend and patron, allowed him to express his clairvoyance in several of his orders, such as Colonia Güell's crypt and Güell Park. Both became an experimenting ground where the laws of Nature could service architecture. The successful result could be materialised on a monumental scale in his greatest work.

Today, when we raise our gaze to the vaults' interior we discover a forest, and amid the tree-like columns, sky light. And if we look at the whole, we admire the recreation of the universal Church. Each bell tower is an apostle, each corner a biblical passage, and each carved stone silently talks to us about God.

But Gaudi, aware that such a sublime design would take several generations to culminate, wanted to build one of the façades before the walls or the roof. In this way his contemporaries would be able to enjoy a finished space and get an idea of the magnitude of the monument, which would also constitute an incentive for the sanctuary's continuity.

THE NAVES

The basilica's general floor plant is a latin cross with three façades. The eastern one is dedicated to the Nativity, the Birth of the Redeemer, the western one to his Passion and Ascension and in front of the sea we find the one dedicated to his Glory. Gaudi could contemplate totally free from scaffolding only the first of the

four bell towers, Saint Barnaba's, which impressively presented his "New Architecture", on November 30 1925. After showing his satisfaction, he added: *"it displeases me not to be able to make just one complete section of the projected naves"*.

Gaudí made two models of the naves and the roofs. The first neo-gothic solution, from 1915, was substituted by one that included hyperbolic paraboloids in 1917. The third and final solution, completed eighty-five years later, finally fulfils his dream.

Due to Gaudí's often insistent wishes, upon entering the basilica one should be able to get a complete view of the great

The Sagrada Familia is a communion of a genius' art with Christian faith. Unlike all the other great temples, it only has one altar.

Next page:
The rigging supports the temple's vaults in an impossible architectural display.

hyperboloid from the presbytery —the biggest in the world, made using the *"volta catalana"* technique—, which is 75m high and features the image of God the Creator clad in a sky blue cape and a huge Venetian mosaic made of gold as the symbol that presents the **"Fiat lux"** —let there be light—, the Creator's first act.

From the heptagonal canopy, which symbolises the gifts of the Holy Spirit, hang 50 lamps and, in the middle, the Saviour crucified. Words of Glory grow amid the bunches of grapes and the sprigs —the wine and bread from the Eucharist—.

The altar, a imposing monolithic block of Iranian porphyry, rises in the middle.

The leaning columns achieve an equilibrium of forces, which let the architect avoid the use of an exterior frame of buttresses that is so characteristic of gothic style.

The enormous space of the presbytery, which holds 300 officiating priests, was presided by His Holiness Benedict XVI on November 7 2010 in the *"urbi et orbi"* consecration of the basilica. Meanwhile, the thousands of devoted voices alternated with those of a thousand choristers who were placed surrounding the temple's great nave, transmitting in unison the celebration of the Eucharist that Gaudí had planned.

The images illustrating this book show his genius and allow us to assure that they answer to the wishes with which he opened the road to follow in his "New Architecture", a style that was partly developed within the Modernist period and that is different from all the others. This unique work attracts people from all over the world because it is the radiance of the Truth, and it conveys the message from Jesus of Nazareth, who came to give testimony of it, in spaces and volumes organised in a way that take us to supreme beauty. This beauty attracts us with such irresistible force that if it wasn't real it would be unexplainable. Like a miracle! A clamour towards universal fraternity in favour of Peace.

It is important to point out that 42 years passed, from the moment when Gaudí accepted the job to build the Sagrada Familia until his death, and the slow growth of the building allowed him to carefully study the solutions to the problems that came up along the way, in a logical process of improvement that led the way.

Gaudí used to say: *"In the Sagrada Familia everything is providential"*. And an important anonymous donation received shortly after the crypt was opened for worship made it possible *"to be able to keep up with the project in a way previously unforeseen. Then the work was given the magnificence that it would have*

otherwise lacked", this is how Mr. César Martinell described it in his book about "Gaudí y la Sagrada Familia". Thanks to that, Gaudí presented a monumental neogothic draft. It went from one bell tower to eighteen. Madness!

GLORY FAÇADE

His last creation, the design of the Glory façade, answers to these words: *"Glory is light, light provides joy, and joy is the happiness of the spirit"*.

For this yet to be built part of the temple Gaudí left an extraordinary volume study from a combination of intertwined hyperboloids. These will form an atrium

Imposing bronze gates open in the Glory façade. They boast the Lord's Prayer carved in 50 languages.

Saint Jordi, patron saint of Catalonia, presides over the nave's feet. He is unarmed, inside the temple there is no room for attacks. That's why he is only holding his shield, which symbolises defence against evil.

Nature's language is masterly represented by the forms and the light.

that will cover the main entrance. Its four bell towers will be similar to the existing eight, but taller and bigger in their diameter.

Eight columns will present the Beatitudes giving way to seven gates that symbolise the seven sacraments and the seven petitions in the Lord's Prayer, the way to reach glory.

Gaudí solved the level difference of 5m between the basilica's pavement and Mallorca street by planning an entrance bridge from a great square that will reach Diagonal avenue.

In the inside of the façade side balconies will be opened for the singers, and it will hold the representation of humanity from its origins with Adam and Eve to its end with work and virtue to reach Glory.

Saint Mary Queen will be surrounded by saints, and Jesus Christ, with the symbols of his Passion and angels announcing the Final Judgement. At the top we will find God the Father and the Holy Ghost. This will undoubtedly be the most impressive entrance to the temple and its main gate, made in bronze by Subirachs, has engravings of The Lord's Prayer in 50 different languages.

THE CRYPT

Excavated under the presbytery, the crypt was the first part to be built in the great monument. When Gaudí accepted the order after the preceding architect had renounced, he made some successful changes to the it, particularly in its access through two lateral staircases instead of a central one that would keep the faithful far

from the altar. In the same way, he planned a surrounding ditch that would improve its ventilation and illumination, and he raised the ribbed vault that rests on the thick columns like a huge shell.

The furniture and the numerous liturgical elements that decorate this room with Gaudí's unmistakable style are worth mentioning. Many of them were made by the architect himself advised by his doctor, as exercising his skilled hands helped him fight rheumatism.

Seven chapels dedicated to the Sagrada Familia of Jesus flank the apse's

perimeter. On the Gospels side we find the chapels of Saint Elizabeth and Saint Zachary. They are followed by the ones dedicated to Saint Joachim and the Immaculate Conception. In the middle we find the chapel of Saint Joseph, the first room of the temple where mass was officiated at the request of Bocabella, fervent devotee of the saint on March 19 1885, despite the fact that the crypt still lacked a roof. On its left we find he one dedicated to Jesus' more earthly side, with the Sacred Heart followed by Saint Anne —the Virgin's mother— and Saint John *the Baptist*.

At the front, the main altar boasts a magnificent bas-relief of the Sagrada Familia, and it is flanked by minor chapels devoted to the Saint Sacrament and the Virgin of Montserrat. On the right, the chapel of Saint Christ holds the remains of the temple's founder, José Mª Bocabella. And on the left side, the chapel of Our Lady of Mount Carmel watches over the Gaudí's sepulchre, which rests at its feet.

With the stained glasses' reflections, the powerful organ is the voice of the temple.

Right:
A giant clam dispenses holy water in the crypt.

Next page:
The crypt, with its byzantine atmosphere, houses jewels like Saint Joseph's Chapel or Gaudi's tomb.

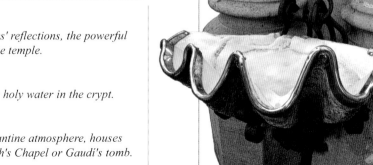

On the shadow of the towers, the Schools used to offer education to the children of the temple's workers. The building, also designed by Gaudí, was a vanguardist model both in its structure and its aesthetics.

THE SCHOOLS

The Construction Board decided to build a school with three classrooms next to the sanctuary in order to solve the neighbourhood's schooling problem. In a few months Gaudí built a 200 square meter nave that used conoids on the roof and on the shaft walls. A simple an economical solution that gained him praise and admiration from the most important rationalist architects of his time. A sketch by Le Corbusier, who visited the building site shortly after Gaudí's death, turned the building into a myth. Sadly, a mob set fire to the building and destroyed it on July 20 1936, as it systematically happened across Republican territory.

The school was restored during the Civil War, even though most of the original building had been lost. Nevertheless, it could be fully reconstructed reusing those original parts which were still in good condition.

Loyal recreation of the original interior.

Thanks to that, we can still see the building as it was planned, as numerous photographs from the time show.

THE MUSEUM

Shortly after Gaudi's death, the general director of Barcelona's Art Museums, Mr. Joaquin Folch, expressed his idea of building a museum centred around the architect's works and locating it in what once used to be his study and workshop. This place was known as "el obrador" and inside it were stored sketches and plaster cast models.

Unfortunately, the blow of the Civil War managed to turn into ashes the great

invaluable treasure of plans, sketches, photographs and models of the genius during the tumultuous month of July in 1936. The plans for the museum changed. The new priority was to reconstruct the battered plaster cast models so that the works could carry on according to Gaudi's wishes. Now we can admire those elements on a monumental scale, materialised in the temple itself.

The first museum opened its doors in 1961 and it has been expanded several times until it reached its current state. Now a didactic exhibition shows the history of the building as well as the creative architectural innovation. The so-called polyfunicular hanging model of Colonia Güell's Crypt constitutes a brilliant example. In it, little bags filled with pellets according to the load they had to support trace the structure's arches in a natural way.

Today walking between its displays, the liturgical furniture and the old photographs and through the model of the main nave feels like walking by the hand of Gaudi himself.

Nativity façade

The Holy Family, sculptural ensemble by Jaume Busquets, was placed in the Nativity façade in 1958.

Right:
A band with Jesus' genealogy wraps the central column that supports the Nativity scene.

Oriented towards sunrise in a clear allusion to the birth of life, this façade looks like a giant Christmas card carved in stone. One whose making took over thirty years. The trumpet angels announce to the world that the Saviour has been born and a stallion of life runs across the iconography to the point that even the birds seem to emerge from the rock.

Practically built by Gaudí, it represents the Mystery of the Incarnation of the Son of God the Father in several episodes that represent the joy of the Creation by the Birth of the Redeemer. A monumental Nativity scene that includes, over the central column, the names of Jesus' human ge-nealogy, from Abraham to Jesus, Mary and Joseph.

Three gates dedicated to the three Christian virtues open themselves to the temple. On the left, a column with Joseph's name carved on it is held by a sea turtle that indicates that this portico, the one devoted **to Hope**, faces the sea. Under a rock from Montserrat, Saint Joseph sitting on a boat is shown as the patron saint of the Catholic church, while a series of passages fills every inch of stone with symbolism: the Flight to Egypt, Saint Joseph's family, the Nile's domestic fauna, or the most dramatic of all: the Slaughter of the Innocents.

The main portico, devoted **to Charity,**

The Coronation of Mary is located in front of the rose window. All the symbolism is complimented by the stained glass windows from the inside.

Left page:
Under the towers, which rise like tubes from a colossal organ, the façade is a stone hymn to Jesus' birth.

Next page:
Saint Joseph sits down holding the church's rudder, next to Saint Barnabas, who lends his name to the tower.

presents over its column, as a capital, the scene that gives its name to this house of God: the "Holy Family". Mary and Joseph wrap up the Child in a basket made in the Catalan tradition, while the mule and the ox warm him up with their breath.

A great Bethlehem star over them seems to shine on the whole iconographic richness, whose symbology is complemented in the stained glass. On the top level there are earthly narratives of the Adora-

tion of the Three Wise Men with their present and the Adoration of the shepherds, carved by Joaquim Ros.

Mary's column flanks the portico **of Faith** and rests on an earth turtle, since this one looks towards the mountain. The virgin appears in several cavities, from which the top one stands out. She is standing over a lamp that symbolises that she is the bearer of life; Jesus' life.

The façade is a great altarpiece, a gigantic sculpture that commemorates the Holy Night of Nativity.

Top:
Young Jesus works at his father's carpentry workshop.

Left page:
Celestial angels adorn the great event with the smell of incense, while the birds seem to be flying away from the stone itself.

In the Adoration of the Shepherds, sculptor Joaquim Ros used a dog to represent loyalty, a lamb to represent docility and the kid's Catalan cap to represent tradition.

The Slaughter of the Innocents shows one of Herodes' soldier's cruelty while a mother begs for mercy for her newborn baby.

Each portico holds a concavity on which entrance we find icicles and snow that remind us that everything we are contemplating took place on a cold December night. In their interiors we admire the wedding of Mary and Joseph, the Coronation of the Virgin by her own son, the Annunciation and the Presentation of Jesus in the temple.

The centre is dominated by a monumental cypress. "The Tree of Life", always green, always pointing towards the sky. Leaning on its trunk, two staircases symbolise the effort it takes to reach virtue. And right at the top, the letter Tau, Greek initial of the word "God", is hugged by a cross, the Son, and the dove of the Holy Ghost. The pigeon doves that fly around it are white souls going to heaven.

To make this elaborated iconography Gaudí surrounded himself by great artists from his time. Later Japanese sculptor Etsuro Sotoo started working on it in 1978.

The angel with the harp was his first statue, made after he had spent hours observing the expressions and hand positions of harpists. Sotoo thinks each work of art is alive because, in the same way as a book tells a different story to each reader, sculptures do the same to each person that looks at them. Because of this, his harp has no strings; we all need to add our own in order to make it sound.

The harpist angel joins his music to that of other angels made by Japanese sculptor Etsuro Sotoo.

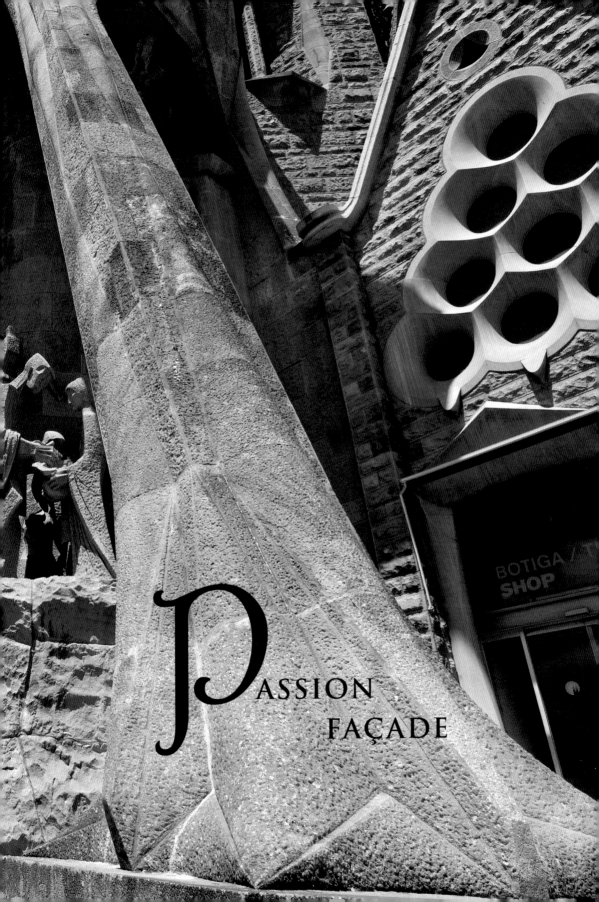

PASSION FAÇADE

At the Crucifixion's feet we find Adam's skull, for whose sin Christ gave his life on the cross.

Right page:
Under the giant bones that structure the façade, the sculptor Subirachs marked each scene with its corresponding biblical signature.

Facing **West,** where the sun also dies, rises the imposing Passion façade.

Gaudí only made an extraordinary sketch of this front, that tells the story from Jesus's triumphal entry into Jerusalem, where he was acclaimed by the people, to his Passion and Death and, at the top, his Ascension.

Naked from ornaments, he left his successors the task of rising it with help of paraboloids, and he trusted that they would be faithful to his ideas. It was built between 1955 and 1976 under direction from architects Quintana, Puig Boada and Bonet Garí. Gaudí said both façades should show a great degree of emotional contrast, between the joy of the Birth of the Redeemer and the cruelty of his Crucifixion.

Sculptor Josep Mª Subirachs was chosen for the job, and he sculpted a monumental façade with contemporary sculptures. While the figures on the opposite façade present mostly round shapes on which light softly slips and sweetens their expressions, here characters show angular features on whose edges light breaks to provoke darkness in a game of shadows that stress the piece's dramatic quality.

Six colossal bones underpin the great stage that houses the fourteen *Stations of the Cross*. On the cornice, 18 additional bones will crown the façade, and the 24 together —the same number of ribs in the human body— will symbolise the crucified torso. A huge frontal shows the names of patriarchs and prophets who await resurrection, which is also represented on the leaded glass window that can be seen from the inside.

The fourteen passages are a story set in stone about the last moments of Jesus' life, and they must be read from bottom to top. The first level recreates the night before his crucifixion. On the left, the **"Last Supper"** shows the disciples' commotion when they learn about their master's death. In **"Peter's confrontation with the soldiers"** we must highlight the ear cut off from the

Roman soldiers present the "Ecce Homo", crowned by thorns, to the people.

Left page:
Like a great parchment paper, the doors of the Gospel narrate the last moments of Jesus' life in bronze.

A faceless Veronica shows the Veil on which Jesus' face is printed.

high priest. The **"Kiss of Judas"** recreated the apostle's betrayal while Jesus was praying in the garden of Gethsemane.

Alone in the middle, **"Jesus tied to the column"** welcomes those who enter the basilica through the bronze gates, in a beautiful allusion to the Word.

On the right it is followed by **"Peter's Denial"**, symbolised by three women, one for each time when he affirmed not to know him before the rooster sang. Peter finds himself allegorically wrapped up in his own guilt.

In the introduction of the **"Ecce Homo"** to the people, Jesus looks melancholic, while Pontius Pilatus looks thoughtful

Top: *Pilatus, saddened by the events.*

Right: *Jesus tied to the column presides the façade in a sculptural ensemble full of symbolism. Over the mullion, alpha and omega. The door, like two sheets of parchment, narrates the Passion in 9,890 bronze letters. The column, made out of four parts, evokes Gaudí's typical crosses. And sculpted with great naturalism, the knot represents oppression and punishment, while the reed, the mocking sceptre that Jesus was given as king of the Jews.*

because of his acts. In the scene of "**Jesus' Judgement**" Pilatus washes his hands, leaving the people to deliver judgement.

The next level up recalls the way to calvary. On the left, "**centurion Longino**" rides a horse while holding the spear that he would use to pierce Jesus' side. In the central recreation of "**Saint Veronica**", Subirachs paid homage to Gaudí twice: sculpting his profile from a photograph, the architect is incarnated in the figure of the evangelist who told about Jesus'

death; and the soldiers' helmets were inspired by the chimneys in La Pedrera. Thanks to the sculptor's genius the Veil of Veronica has been emptied in the shroud, like a negative, and he left Veronica faceless so that she would not take attention away from Jesus' face.

"**The Encounter with the three Marys**" shows Simon helping him to stand up from his third fall while the three Marys —Mary of Clopas, Mary Magdalene and his own mother the Virgin— stare in sadness.

Peter, wrapped in his own guilt for having denied Jesus three times before the rooster sang.

The upper level is a great sacrifice altar that narrates Jesus' own death. On the left, **"the Soldiers gamble for Jesus' clothes"** on a table that looks like a four-sided ankle bone that was used in a game that can be considered the precursor of dice games.

The main scene shows **"Jesus crucified"** in front of John and Mary, who are disconsolate. At the cross' feet rests Adam's skull, symbol of the sin Jesus gave his life for. At the top, the Easter moon incarnates the night, and the sepulchre's door is empty.

On the right we find **"the Entombment"**. Joseph of Arimathea and Nicodemus wrap up Jesus' body in the shroud, while on the background the Virgin looks at them and prays. And at the top, on the bridge that joins the towers, **"Christ resurrected"** does not occupy the central part, for He *"is sitting at the right hand of the Father"*.

The two façades close the transept and establish a dialogue between themselves. One cannot exist without the other; Birth and Death, Nativity and Easter, just as the Sagrada Familia's master wanted.

QUOTES BY GAUDÍ

"THE ARCHITECT OF THE FUTURE WILL BASE HIS WORK ON THE IMITATION OF NATURE, BECAUSE IT'S THE MOST RATIONAL, LASTING AND ECONOMICAL OF METHODS".

"MY IDEAS ARE OF INDISPUTABLE LOGIC; THE ONLY THING THAT MAKES ME DOUBT IS THE FACT THAT THEY HAVE NEVER BEEN APPLIED BEFORE".

"ORIGINALITY CONSISTS OF THE RETURN TO THE ORIGIN. THEREFORE, SOMETHING ORIGINAL IS THAT WHICH GOES BACK TO THE SIMPLICITY OF THE FIRST SOLUTIONS".

"DO YOU WANT TO KNOW WHERE I FOUND MY MODEL? IN TREES. A TREE GROWS UPWARDS, IT SUPPORTS ITS BRANCHES, WHICH SUPPORT THEIR TWIGS, WHICH SUPPORT THEIR LEAVES. AND EACH INDIVIDUAL PART HAS BEEN GROWING IN HARMONY AFTER GOD, THE ARTIST, CREATED THEM".

"TO GOD, THE GREATEST IS NOT THE DIMENSIONAL, BUT THE PERFECT".

"THE STRAIGHT LINE IS THE LINE OF MEN, BUT THE CURVE IS THE LINE OF GOD".

"EVERYTHING COMES OUT OF THE GREAT BOOK OF NATURE; MEN'S WORKS ARE ALREADY A PRINTED BOOK".

"ARTISTS SHOULDN'T HAVE MONUMENTS MADE BECAUSE THEY ARE ALREADY MADE OUT OF THEIR WORK".

"THE TEMPLE OF THE SAGRADA FAMILIA WILL REPRESENT THE FUTURE OF MODERN CATALONIA".

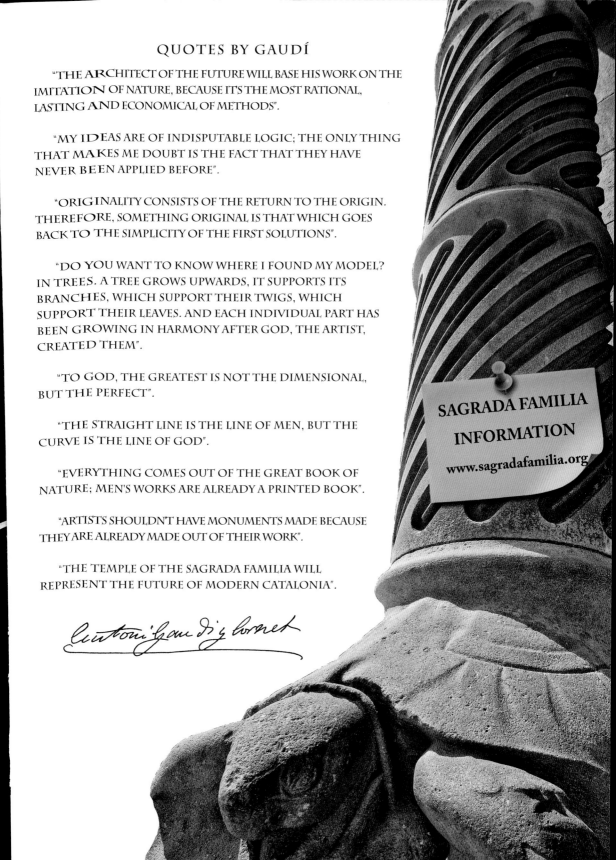

SAGRADA FAMILIA
INFORMATION
www.sagradafamilia.org

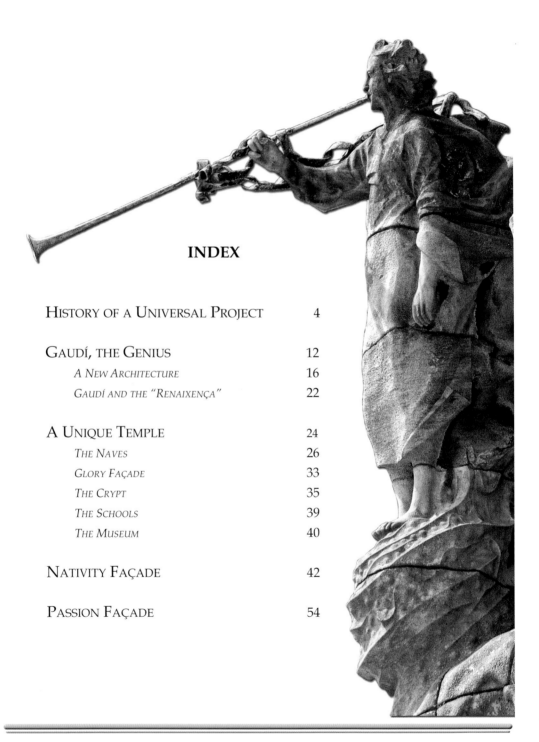

INDEX